Knuckle Bear

Poems by Tim Peeler

Shawnee, Oklahoma

Several of these poems have or will appear in *Kentucky Review* and *Wild Goose Poetry Review*. Thanks to those editors.

Cover Art and Design: Jack Wells Dickson
Author Photo: Penny Abernethy Peeler
Interior Design: Smythtype Design

Red Dirt Press
1530 N. Harrison Street #143
Shawnee, Oklahoma 74804

www.redtruckreview.com/press.shtml

ISBN-13: 978-1511755955

In Memory of John Billy Baird

Contents

Knuckle Bear 1

Ain't nobody gonna kill no mockingbird around here.
I got the fence all outlaid around the woods,
Drived the stuck stakes deep between the trees,
And now I'm on the porch in Granny's swing
Watching the traffic heavy up when the mills let
And I know about everyone comes by waving
In their rattletrap trucks, shiny unfordable cars,
Last year I had a bone graph on my leg
Said it was all them sundrops cause it.
If I could have one thing it would be
That young girl drive the bug with sunglasses
Only one come by not smoking Winston.
Granny tole me how they killed the mockingbird
Alabama someres and I seized on it.
Papaw lef all them postes in second shed
And wire he stole from the mill I said
Granny, ain't nobody gonna kill no mockingbird
Around here I am good with hands
So I found the one sledge still on a handle
And I am not afeared of copperheads
That bit Papaw's blue tic on the balls.
I like the way that young girl drive
And look at herself in the mirror twicely.
The light dances on her I say Yeah
Like the preacher say slobberin
On his bible the spirt fixin to dance him.
Papaw always call me Knuckle Bear
Or just Knuck when he want me
To do something for em.

Knuckle Bear 2

Papaw say Knuckle Bear, when you
Gonna about never do something,
And I say nothing much and
He slap me and say, Knuck, get in that truck.
Papaw socks got gold toes
Some of these days I think
Papaw the preacher
Way he tell me get in the truck.
Granny sing me in the kitchen
When the grease pop, she go Owl
And rub her red apron,
Knuckle Bear, she say, I ain't
Never gonna let that bad man
Take you. Granny let me
Lick the beater we had Eastern cupcakes
For Jesus and his bunny eggs
Granny say Daddy gonna eat
But Mommy got her children
Someers else today
Jesus is in the sky on the cross
Left his clothes in a cave.

Knuckle Bear 3

I love that one mile walk
Down to the river up the hill
To the ball field
Papaw say Knuckbear
Gonna make you a ball player
And I swing Papaw throw
Fast hard hit me I say Owl
Papaw say you so big boy
And I swing wraparound
And I swing hit way yonder
Papaw don't say nothing
Then he say good Lord Knuck
And we look for a hour
In the kazoo out past grass
Till Papaw step on her
In the long sun
My shadow longer than his'n
When you hit it run he say
Some days Papaw put me out there
With people and it felt so good
When I hit I forget the run part.

Knuckle Bear 4

Granny tune my heart
With her kitchen song.
Run from us, God, run from us,
I think, when Papaw line a rabbit
With his twenty-two, but
How I like barbcue.
Papaw has two trucks
He drive whichever crank first.
He say come on Knuckle Bear.
I load a truck with chair.
They play cards in the house,
Beard men with guns.
Outside I hear hawgs snuffling.
The wind is dead.
Papaw say bust that fucker.
I knock him out front door
Backwards off the porch.
Papaw scoop the table money,
Give me a quarter.
Granny tune my heart
With Rock and Ages
After we go fucker bustin.

Knuckle Bear 5

Papaw say don't never live past yourself.
He fell and hit his dead.
Papaw say older you get
More you like old stuff.
Granny say they bury him in the bone orchard
Where he waits for Jesus.
Some day I go check to see if he there.
Papaw never good at waiting.
Papaw cuff me and say Knuckle Bear
You slow as a day at work.
Then cousin Ettie Lay say Knuckle Bear
You dumber than pig shit.
She like me, put her hand down my pants
Behind the barn while I watch the bull
Lick grain and snot from his nose.
Then I say wee, she let go and laugh.

Knuckle Bear 6

I like snakes, look wet feel dry.
Papaw catch the copperhead
Say it the one kill Blue
Put it in paceboard box
One he fetch grocery in
Tape it with duck tape
Put at end of garden
By dry up squash plants
We sit listen snake hiss
Strike end of box
Then Papaw pour gas
Scratch match against his zipper
Then pow the fire shoot
Taller than the corn stalks
And he say Knuckle Bear
Pay attention for oncet
That how you turn a
Copperhead into a black snake.

Knuckle Bear 7

Papaw say it ain't a lie if you believe it.
Granny say theys too much lying everwhere.
The Lord does not speak to me.
I listen to the darkness.
I listen to the neighbor chain dog barking.
I listen to the old truck climb the hill.
I listen to the city lights down there.
I listen to the walnut tree yawn.
I listen to the rabbit grass.
The Lord passes close to my ear,
Does not speak to me.
I am Knuckle Bear. Not a lie.

Knuckle Bear 8

Football just like fucker bustin.
I like the helmet. I like the cleat.
They say lean here; hit that one.
Move when everbody move.
They hit me. It feel good, not like Papaw
Slappin my leg with a briar stalk.
They holler damit, Knuckle Bear
 When I hit wrong one.
Then I can't tell who who.
Hit the black one. They all black.
White boy, black shirt. Black boy, white shirt.
All crazy everwhere.
Then I hit the whistle man.
Bust that fucker good.

Knuckle Bear 9

October night lights
Over yonder get brighter.
I smell the leafs fall.
Cross the river I hear that train.
Morning Granny send me tidy Papaw grave.
I sit there on gray hump clip yeller grass.
Papaw never say Knuckle Bear get them weeds.
Never say Knuckle Bear where yore hoe.
Never say Knuckle Bear I wanna show you something.
Never say Knuckle Bear fetch me a beer, my paper,
Fat head screw dryer, 7/16 ranch,
Switch, hanky, grease gun, ax.
I trace finger in his cold name
Papaw dead for shore.

Ettie Lay 1

It's the little things that matter.
Old Man ask me to take a shower
When he gonna eat me up.
I get in there run the water hot
Wash slow make him wait
Skip them parts down there though
So the sweat and grime of the raw day stay;
Then I get out lotion my legs breasts
Pee and barely wipe.
It's the little things.

Ettie Lay 2

Knuckle Bear had a wanger
Big like everything else about him,
Long and flat and wide at the head
like a airplane propeller.
I'd pull it out in the barn loft
Or behind the woodshed
When everbody was in the house
Watching Bonanza or Andy Griffin.
He act like he didn't want me to
And I'd talk mean to him while I did it
So he didn't get the wrong idea.

Ettie Lay 3

I could barely get that thing in my mouth
And the first time I did it, he run off
Across the field down into the woods.
He look like a big foot loping along
Running a little sideways.
Lord knows what Papaw
Had done to that boy.
Next Sunday we visit
He found me in the woods
Waiting for him of course.
He pushed my head down there
And I did it just like Sis told me
Taste like water at Myrtle Beach.
Knuckle Bear moaned and tremble
And I knew I had him.

Ettie Lay 4

Old Man says I'm the sweetest thing
He ever taste. The fat round his waist
Shakes and he got tities now
Not like the man I marry.
He don't know nothing.
I might be poisonin him.
I might be fuckin the preacher.
I might be doin about anything,
But the fact is
That I ain't doin nothing at all.

Ettie Lay 5

Three Sundays went by
Without a visit to Papaw's.
Then we go I'm wearing
My tightest jeans blouse
Tied above my belly button.
Knuckle Bear followed me
Into the garage behind
All the barrels full of nuts
And bolts and everthing
You could need to fix something.
Then I lay back on some burlap
Struggled out of those jeans
And panties all the time
Telling him this is how
It's going to be
If you want my mouth.

Ettie Lay 6

I said Knuckle Bear
It like you got the beater
With the cake icing on it.
You know they ain't much
And how good it taste
So you lick it real slow
Till I tell you fast.
He tried to pull that thing out
But I said put that dick up
Till we through here,
And he did.

Ettie Lay 7

I smelled the motor oil
And the rusty saws
Hanging on the wall
And the musty dirt
Under the gravel
And the kerosene can
In the corner even
The old empty feed sacks
And I felt the vibration
Of the earth turning.
Get off I hollered
Momma was standing
Behind him.

Ettie Lay 8

Momma slapped Knuck,
Not really hard, no mark.
Shushed us both.
I pulled my pants up
Tears running down my face.
I'm not gonna tell Papaw
She said if yall listen to me.
Then she laid down
On that burlap
Rised up her Sunday dress
Spread her fat legs
And made Knuck do her.
That when it all got unreally.

Papaw 1

His crazy mother my worthless daughter
Left him with us when he was four,
Anything to keep him away from his daddy,
And then those brothers.
We'd already done our raisin
But we prayed over it and the answer
Was the pure honesty of the boy,
Never know nothing and never would
But he'd never lie ye.
Knuckle Bear I'd say and he come to me
Like a big ole dog waitin for a bone.

Papaw 2

I look at him see my mother's eyes,
My nose and chin, I look at him and see blood.
I know he special, I know he hard to take.
I heard all that. I listen to my daughter cry
Yet she won't tell me what his daddy done.
I see her mark up, lip split, black eye,
I put my arm around her to hug she wince
Say she fell down the steps again.
Next Saturday we invite Knuck daddy
To the poker house he all lit up
Slappin the boys on the back
Talking shit about big money
How he gonna start his own side bizness
Who he gonna whup next.
Before the night over
He beggin on his knees.

Papaw 3

Most days I work the farm,
Keep fifty sixty head, some hawgs,
Chicken, sell hay, put up hay, fix fence,
Trade at the store, some days
I fix stuff for the mill boss,
Not the kind of fixin you think.
Move dawdlers outta houses,
Move new one in. Boss say
 Don't want that en no more.
Back my truck up start throwin
Their shit in the yard.
Another en in fore the sun
Fall into the river.

Papaw 4

Sometimes they cry
Children pitiful dirty as rats.
I say Knuck lets step it up.
He move like the place on fire.
That boy can flat throw
Somebody's shit into the yard.
Boss pay cash always
Get Granny a new apron
Red white check she like
Buy Knuck a big cord of licorish
He work all day like a grown man
For candy.

Papaw 5

One day the boss call
Say you know what you gotta do
Long story short
Old Man Jacumin sell bad licker
To the mill hands poisnin
Missin work, still owe debt
At the store never pay
I know them woods
Out back his barn
Sneak through the dark
Like a haint.

Papaw 6

I look through open door
He sittin gainst a stack
Of grain sacks goat drunk
Never hears nothing
In the flickering fire light
I see the shadow
Of my raised hammer
Watch the shadow
Like it doin
The hard deed
Not me.

Papaw 7

Never kill a man
If you can't leave three ways
I pour the shine here there
Quick in the moonlight silver
Scratch and flick a match
On the line I drawed from the yard
Then ran past where
I snuffed his dog
Into darkness I knowed
Better than the day.

Papaw 8

Next day paper say
You could see the fire
From three counties
Sherriff and the Boss
Talkin on the TV
Say Jacumin pass out smokin
His still blow up
Real tragedy
Say he a good man.

Ettie Lay 9

Papaw found out, don't know how,
Knuck or Momma, it didn't matter.
We go over next Sunday,
Park the car under a maple,
Windy, yeller leafs snowflaking
Around Papaw where he stand
Waiting, motion for Momma
Roll the window down.
He say you stay in the car,
Pointing his huge gnarl finger
At Momma.

Ettie Lay 10

Papaw take me out to metal shed
Next to the barn, push me through
The door, shut it behind him.
He reach up pull the light string.
It flicker then come on hard
So I could see his red face, white beard.
Papaw, I'm sorry, I say,
And though I was just fourteen
I still feel those words leave my mouth.

Ettie Lay 11

He push me forward
I hear his boots on the sorry wood floor,
My floppers stopping then where
He stand me against two saw horses.
Pull em down he say
But my hands shake so much
I can't do the button.
He reach rough around me
Pull my jeans to the floor
Then my panties after.
I'm a little rouse but not the good kin'
The kin' you about to piss yourself.

Ettie Lay 12

He lean me cross the sawbuck
Then say grab that other en.
I reach and take hold of it,
Get up on your toes he say
And if you move a muscle
Or say a word gonna be worse.
I get on my toes and I feel
Like when I was little
Walking around in Momma's heels
Except this hurt to burn.
Then I hear him stobbing
With a hoe to free
The bullwhip from its hook.

Ettie Lay 13

I'm thinkin I ain't never been bullwhipped
And I try to look back under my arm
To see what he's a doin
And my left foot come flat
Get on them toes he say
And I hear him splat the grease gun
On an oily rag. It so still
I can hear the rag slide
Up and down the whip as he works it.

Ettie Lay 14

My legs burn extra hot
So I don't think I can stand it no more.
I smell him and it ain't lust,
Thinking about my bare raise ass.
I already knowed that smell.
And I was sure he was tryin
To decide if he was gonna kill me.
Everbody knowed he kill Knuck's
Daddy and fed him to the hogs.

Ettie Lay 15

I tried to pray
But already I didn't believe nothin then.
Outside it start to rain,
Great drops splatting on the tin roof.
I felt a cold drop leak and hit
Just above my butt bone,
Another, another
And then I let loose
Pee runnin yeller down my leg
Papaw please hit me now I say.

Ettie Lay 16

Get you pants up he say
And I'm reachin and pullin
And turnin all at once
And fixin to run
When he grab me by the face.
Hold my whole face
Between his thumb and first finger
And say you git back out to that car
And ifin you and you momma
Every come back here
Or mess with that boy
I will finish this
And he stick the butt end of the whip
Right up against my teeth.

Ettie Lay 17

That's the last I see Knuck up close
For a long long time.
But I think about him a lot
And Papaw till they faces blur
Into one fuzzy memory
And I wonder if folks
Ever get what they deserve
And if he had whupped me
That day maybe
I'd a turn out a better woman.

Knuckle Bear 10

I am not afeared of deaf.
Papaw say it only sleep
Granny say it waiting for Jesus.
I set out for boneyard
With a shovel want to see Papaw
Granny call church
Preacher say Knuckle Bear
Stay out the boneyard.
When I think Papaw now
I go set the truck
Wait for Papaw to crank it
Take me to Jesus too.

Knuckle Bear 11

Papaw gone
Granny gone
Boss gone
Mill gone
Young girl
With heart shape glasses gone
Cows gone
Knuck still here.

Knuckle Bear 12

Church ladies bring food
I sit porch watch road
Can't walk good no more
Barbcue chicken pie
Corn slaw sweet tea
They say Knuck
Jesus love you
We do too hug me
Smell like flower
Cousin brother call me
Say I don't leave
They gonna burn the place down.

Knuckle Bear 13

I go to store
Like Papaw say
Put on tab
Get sundrop beanie weenie
Pot meat crackers
Lickerish soap
Anything else
Young girl say
Not young girl in the bug
This one tired
Smoke Winston.

Papaw 9

People say I hard on him,
But I knowed what the world would do
I done my share of bad too
And I look at Knuck and know
He the chance the Lord give me
To square my deal.

Papaw 10

Everybody know me round here
Most of them owe me some way
So I set about some fixin of my own.
I dug up that filthy lucre
Here and there
You don't need to know where.
Sold the bottom
Halved the herd
Hired that neighbor boy
What went away and
Become a lawyer
Fixed it for Granny
When I'm gone
Fixed it for Knuck.

Papaw 11

I went to see them brothers.
All high settin on they porch.
What you want old man
Say the fat one
Chewin on a straw.
I'm a leavin the place to Knuck
But y'all know that sure.
Just want you know
When I'm gone
A badder man than me
Will be watchin'.

Papaw 12

What make you think
We gonna let you leave
This porch alive
The skin one say
His face look like a skull
Enough stretch over it
To make him just alive.
I got my hand on my hawk
Lookin at they belly button
Cause a man can't move
Without it.

Papaw 13

I cut you throat
Before you get you gun
Out of that belt I say.
He look at me
Like he thinkin
He can do it.
I cut you heads off
Feed my hawgs I say.
That lil one try to hold my eyes
Like he a TV bad guy
But I walk back to truck
Never look at em
Like they ain't shit.

Knuckle Bear 14

Church ladies come get me some day
Take me to place smell like old people.
Walk me to where you go three ways.
We go to the middle down the hall
Walk into a room and there Granny.
I say Granny is this heav'n.
I thought you dead.

Knuckle Bear 15

Granny look far about worse
Than last time I thought she dead.
She not fat no more.
Her eyes all wet hands shake.
She say Knuckle Bear I love you
Want to see you one more time.
I say Granny make me some biscuits.
She laugh and cough
Say Knuck you a good boy.
I hug her long time.
Church ladies take me home.
I can't remember.

Knuckle Bear 16

Depady Dawg move across the road.
He bigger than Knuck.
He big as Haws Carright.
He take me for ride to store
Say Knuck let me know
Anytime you need me.
He come set porch
With me sometimes
Got TV workin again
I watch TVland
Ever night.
Them brother cousins
Don't call no more.

Knuckle Bear 17

I can't hardly walk no more.
Set the porch
Watch cars go by.
Don't know where come from.
Don't know nobody no more.
Church ladies bring supper.
Depady bring me sundrop
And lickerish from store.
He wash my clothes.
Sometimes I don't
Get to bathroom.
Somebody come kill
That mockingbird now
Knuck can't stop em.
Can't hold no shotgun.
Can't throw no knife.
Can't bust no fuckers.

Knuckle Bear 18

I set the porch.
I set the porch.
Remember Papaw
Throwin all them pitches.
And I'm just a swingin
Swingin at everone
And this time I hit em
I hit everone
I hit everone
And everbody is so happy
I bust them fuckers good
And I don't forget to run.

ACKNOWLEDGEMENTS

I would like to offer my gratitude to David Dickson, Michel Stone, Ted Pope, Carter Monroe, Tim Earley, Ron Rash, Gary Mitchem, Scott Owens, Keith Flynn, and Mike James who read parts or all of the manuscript in its various stages.

Special thanks to Amy Susan Wilson, Publisher, Red Dirt Press.

42672253R00033

Made in the USA
Charleston, SC
05 June 2015